50
GAMES
TO PLAY WITH
YOUR DOG

50
GAMES
TO PLAY WITH
YOUR DOG

Suellen Dainty

Foreword by Janet Tobiassen, DVM

First published in 2007 by T.F.H. Publications
President/CEO Glen S. Axelrod
Executive Vice President Mark E. Johnson
Publisher Christopher T. Reggio
Production Manager Kathy Bontz
US Editor Heather Russell-Revesz

T.F.H. Publications, Inc. One TFH Plaza
Third and Union Avenues Neptune City, NJ 07753, US

ISBN-13: 978-07938-0617-1

Library of Congress Cataloging-in-Publication Data
Dainty, Suellen.
    50 games to play with your dog / Suellen Dainty.
        p. cm.
    Includes index.
    ISBN-13: 978-0-7938-0617-1 (alk. paper)
    1. Games for dogs. I. Title. II. Title: Fifty games to play with your dog.

    SF427.45.D35 2007
    636.7'0887--dc22   2007017103

This book was conceived, designed, and produced by iBall, an imprint of
Ivy Press
The Old Candlemakers, West Street, Lewes, East Sussex, BN7 2NZ, UK

Creative Director Peter Bridgewater   *Publisher* Jason Hook
Editorial Director Caroline Earle   *Senior Project Editor* Dominique Page
Art Director Sarah Howerd   *Project Designer* Kevin Knight and Suzie Johanson
Designer Ginny Zeal   *Photographer* Nick Ridley
Illustrator Joanna Kerr

This book has been published with the intent to provide accurate and authoritative information in regard to the subject matter within. While every reasonable precaution has been taken in preparation of this book, the author and publisher expressly disclaim responsibility for any errors, omissions, or adverse effects arising from the use or application of the information contained herein. The techniques and suggestions are used at the reader's discretion and are not to be considered a substitute for veterinary care. If you suspect a medical problem consult your veterinarian.

Printed and bound in Thailand
08 09 10 11 5 7 9 8 6 4

The author and publisher would like to thank the following
for permission to reproduce photographs:
© A. Inden/zefa/Corbis, page 110;
© Jupiter Images, page 111 top;
© Waltraud Ingerl/iStockphoto, page 112;
© Lawrence Manning/Corbis, page 113;
© Getty Images, page 114;
© Index Stock Imagery/Photolibrary, page 115 top.
Cover Image: Calvey Taylor-Haw.

The Leader in Responsible Animal Care
for Over 50 Years!™

www.tfh.com

CENTRAL
Garden & Pet

Contents

Foreword

Dogs have always been an important part of my life. From an early age I was actively involved in 4-H; training and showing dogs while learning about anatomy, care, and grooming. Visiting nursing homes as part of pet therapy work, I witnessed the power of the human–animal bond many times over. People who wouldn't speak or interact with others would communicate a wide range of emotions as soon as I brought my dogs and cat to visit.

It was after a car accident that I again realized the value of pets in my life. I had great difficulty walking and my doctor warned me that I might always have a limp. My dogs, however, wouldn't let me forget about their daily walks, no matter how I felt. My doctor was surprised at my progress—no limp. I would probably have given up without my dogs' encouragement. Even though that was many years ago, every day I am grateful to the dogs who have been in my life.

Therefore as someone who loves dogs, and tries to be fit, I very much enjoyed reading *50 Games to Play With Your Dog*. In busy day-to-day life, it's easy to be present without really "being there," both for our pets and for our families. Quality time is often lost to finishing projects and keeping appointments. This book focuses on that quality time and communication—something to be celebrated and enjoyed with our dog companions and family. It offers a wide selection of games for a variety of dog (and people) personalities. You can learn about creative pursuits for curious dogs, such as Buried Treasure and Hide and Seek, find ways to keep active dogs happy with games such as Walkies! and Agility Course Training, and you can appeal to the exhibitionist dog personality with Doggy Dancing and Night Night. These games, and many more, offer a variety of opportunities to discover what your dog truly enjoys.

For those new at dog training, it offers plenty of good background information on dog behavior, plus various training techniques (reward and clicker). The photographs are engaging and the step-by-step instructions are easy to follow. The dogs pictured throughout represent a wide range of breeds and sizes, all of which are clearly having fun with the task at hand.

As a veterinarian, I especially appreciated the tips and safety concerns one must consider before embarking on new training or exercise programs. Awareness of your dog's age, size, agility, and basic likes and dislikes is so important for overall success and for your dog's enjoyment of these games.

This book is the perfect addition to any dog-lover's library. I'm already envisioning the new level of communication that I'll have with my dogs as soon as I put these ideas into practice. Read it. Play games. Your dog will thank you.

Janet Tobiassen, DVM
About.com Guide
www.about.com

Introduction

W hy should you play with your dog? There are several answers, and perhaps the most obvious is also the strongest argument: because you'll both enjoy it! But there are a number of others that it's worth knowing about, because play isn't a trivial matter for dogs—it's important for their overall well-being.

The dog is one of the few animals that plays into adulthood; usually baby animals play to learn survival skills—then, as they mature, turn those games towards the serious adult business of living in the wild. But somewhere along the way, during the thousands of years over which dogs became domesticated, they learned to play into adulthood—and a healthy, properly stimulated pet dog will often play into old age, provided the games are kept appropriate for his fitness level and skills.

Even a self-contained dog values human company, and playing with him shows him that you value the bond with him, too. It's not just fun for a dog, it's also reassuring that you're prepared to interact with him, confirming his role as a team player under your leadership. And dogs who are confident and relaxed about their position in their family "pack" usually behave better outside of the play arena, as well as within it. Extend your dog's play repertoire as far as you and he are able; not only will this keep boredom at bay but it will also stretch him a little. This doesn't mean that you should put a miniature dachshund through a full agility course, simply that you should stretch the boundaries of what you're both used to if your dog seems ready for it. Keep an eye out for signs that your dog has had enough, either mentally or physically, and make sure that you know his physical limitations before you try anything new.

A lot has been written about the human role as "pack leader" and the importance of never allowing your dog to dominate you. This is a complex area that there isn't space to discuss in detail here. But don't get so obsessed with being the leader and the disciplinarian that you can't allow your dog to play freely. Recent research has shown that wild dogs living in packs are highly organized and that their relationships have a great deal of give and take—the group tends to let the individual best suited to a specific task take it on. One bout of energetic Tug shouldn't threaten your authority with your dog, so don't worry too much about your role being compromised. If there are real discipline problems, they're likely to emerge outside of play.

Finally, what's the difference between a game and a trick? This is often asked—sometimes by people who don't like to see a dog doing tricks—and there's only one answer: a game is anything that your dog loves to do and that gives him the opportunity to interact with you or with other dogs. It doesn't matter if an onlooker might call it a trick (and you certainly won't damage the dog's dignity!) just so long as the dog is having fun.

Play Basics

Chances are if you've had your dog since she was a puppy you've probably been playing with her from the moment she joined the household. An adult dog, whether from a shelter or another source, may have taken a little longer to assimilate but chances are that you play with her too. But even if you already play a good deal in a fairly unstructured way don't skip this section. Some of the games in the chapters that follow require your dog to know a few easily taught basics—and you can learn them here if she doesn't already have them down. And be sure to check out the safety advice before you start, too.

How Your Dog Learns

The classic way to teach your dog uses food treats. Most dogs love to eat, so offering food as a reward is usually the best way to introduce any game that involves learning. (Some games, mostly the throwing and catching types, are so instinctive to dogs that you'll find "teaching" them isn't necessary—the game itself is enough motivation.) Rewards should be small—you'll be using a lot of them at first—and special: tiny chunks, about the size of your little fingertip, of dried liver, chicken, or cheese are all usually popular. Offer the treat as both incitement and reward: show it to the dog as a persuader, and give it to him as soon as he's attempted the behavior you're suggesting. Sometimes you'll have to reward a try, because some of the games are hard to learn and the dog will become demotivated if even his best, though unsuccessful, attempt goes unrewarded. Pet and praise your dog as well as treating him; eventually you can phase the treats out as he becomes familiar with a game or trick, and use praise alone.

The important lesson when you're teaching a dog something new is to keep your sessions short and enjoyable. Don't persist with a game that your dog is obviously not enjoying; this is supposed to be fun. Be consistent. If your dog isn't allowed on the furniture, don't let him up on the couch for a game, or you'll confuse him. Don't ever coerce your dog into doing anything that he's plainly uneasy about: this can backfire terribly, and the damage to his confidence could take a long time to repair.

As well as rewards, consider using a clicker. Originally developed to train dolphins, it encourages dogs to work out for themselves what you want. If you offer a reward each time your dog hears a click, you can indicate the behavior you want him to repeat. For example, if you want to teach your dog to lie down, wait until he lies down, click, and offer a reward. Each time he lies down, click and reward. Your dog quickly makes the association and works out what it is that you want him to do.

Picking the Right Game

First things first: you need to know your dog. No one knows your pet like you do; not just what might be expected from his breed and background, but his personal likes and dislikes, his enthusiasms and fears. A lot of generalizing goes on about dog breeds, and much of it may be true: for instance, you might hear that "collies are the smartest, and enjoy all games" or "all terriers love to dig"—and this may be true of most collies and most terriers, and can be a helpful guide if you're not sure what to try first when you're enlarging your pet's play repertoire. Essentially, though, it's like saying "all girls love to play with dolls": generalizations shouldn't blind you to the particular activities the canine member of your family loves the best. Try all of the options, even if they're not naturally highlighted for the breed you own; you may find that you're the first known owner of an agility basset or a scent-trail pug!

Play can build a shy dog's confidence levels and help an uncertain dog to socialize, but the game needs to be the right type—one that reinforces his strengths, not plays to his weaknesses. No dog, especially a strong-minded one, should be allowed to become a play pest, so keep your playtimes special and invite your pet to play rather than give in to his constant nagging. If your dog ever growls or nips in the course of play (and you need to distinguish between the much lower and more serious sound of a canine warning and mere barks, yelps, and whimpers of excitement) stop the game and put the toys away. Don't punish your dog; just stop interacting with him until he's calmed down. Remember your own body language when you're in mid-game. Don't use your height to loom over a dog; a young or small dog may find it intimidating, and a large, self-confident dog could read it as a challenge. Use your tone to stage-manage the game: an excited voice will incite your pet to action, while a low, steady tone may encourage him to stop and think, particularly when he's trying to learn something hard.

Even when you have established a favorite game—or two, or three—introduce a new one now and then to keep your playtime varied and exciting for both of you.

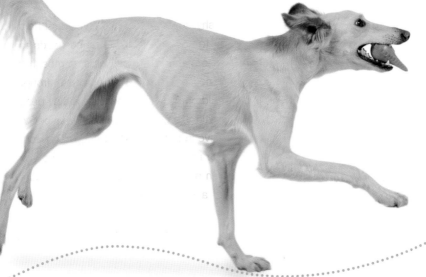

Sit, Stay, and Down

The likelihood is that your dog has already learned these three simple commands. They're the building blocks of every game you will play with her, so it's vital that she understands them clearly before you start. If she doesn't already know, here's how to teach them.

To teach "Sit," stand in front of your dog with a treat. Lift your hand as she comes towards you. As her nose comes up, her rear end will naturally go down. As it starts to move downwards, say "Sit." Reward her as soon as her bottom hits the ground. When she sits every time you ask her, teach "Stay." Put her on a leash (you'll find it's easier), ask her to sit, let her see that you're holding a treat, then slowly move backward, while giving the command "Stay." Move just a couple

of paces, holding the treat in front of her. If she starts to get up, put her back into a sit, and begin again. As soon as she's staying, even for a second or two, give her the treat. Gradually increase the distance you move away, until she will "stay" a fair way away from you. To teach her to lie down, kneel beside your dog while she's sitting. Let her sniff a treat in your hand, then slowly move your hand down in front of her. She'll start to go down, and as she does so give the command "Down." Keep moving the food forward and down; as soon as she's lying down fully, reward and praise her.

Teach all three of these commands for just five minutes every day—but make sure that it *is* every day—and you'll find that your dog quickly gets the hang of them.

Playing Safe

Dogs love playing so much that you can't always expect them to exercise caution. This applies firstly to the game a dog is playing; she may not think about whether it's safe for her to jump at a certain angle, for instance, especially when she's absolutely determined to reach that desirable toy. Secondly, you should consider whether or not it's uncomfortable or even dangerous for her to move in a certain way; very long-backed dogs, for example, such as dachshunds, shouldn't do a lot of high jumping or balancing on their hind legs—they can damage their backs—but they may not remember that, so you have to. You need to be your pet's play monitor, and to judge what's safe and what isn't. The pages that follow carry a few specific warnings relating to specific games, but there are some general points you should take into account when picking appropriate activities for your pet.

Every breed has its strengths and weaknesses: some larger dogs are prone to hip dysplasia and arthritis, other breeds to weak backs, and some of the flatter-faced dogs, such as pekes and pugs, can have difficulty breathing if they're overstretched. Young dogs shouldn't be overexerted while they're still growing, so you may have to be the one to play bad cop and to call time before Buddy is ready to give up. Dogs that are more than five weeks' pregnant, too, shouldn't play anything very energetic. None of this means you shouldn't play with your dog, simply that you need to be mindful of her strengths and weaknesses. If you're doubtful about what's safe, check with your veterinarian about any potential weaknesses you should work around. Old dogs can certainly learn new tricks, but it's best not to overtax them.

Keep an eye, too, on where you play, and with what. Make sure that you're in safe surroundings; if there's balancing to be done, don't work on a slippery surface, and make drinking water freely available. It's best not to play energetically less than an hour before or after your dog has eaten, nor at the hottest part of a hot day. Finally, check anything you give your dog to play with: sharp edges, small parts that could be chewed or swallowed, and painted or chemically treated toys are all no-nos.

That's enough warnings—now go have some fun with your dog!

Fetch Games

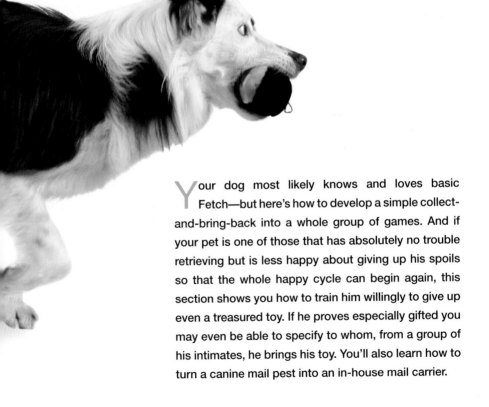

Your dog most likely knows and loves basic Fetch—but here's how to develop a simple collect-and-bring-back into a whole group of games. And if your pet is one of those that has absolutely no trouble retrieving but is less happy about giving up his spoils so that the whole happy cycle can begin again, this section shows you how to train him willingly to give up even a treasured toy. If he proves especially gifted you may even be able to specify to whom, from a group of his intimates, he brings his toy. You'll also learn how to turn a canine mail pest into an in-house mail carrier.

▶ ONE Most dogs will run immediately after a toy or ball that has been thrown. As your dog starts to run, say "Fetch." As she reaches her objective and picks the ball up, praise her.

Return to Sender

Some dog breeds, such as labradors and golden retrievers, seem to be born to play "Fetch" games. Not every dog will be so keen, but Fetch is a great way to double the amount of exercise your dog gets (while you simply stand and throw!), so it's worth persevering until your pet gets the idea. If she's slow to pick it up, keep the session short and move on to something else; it's important that you never bore your pet when playing.

PLAYING FETCH IN WATER

Dogs who like water and who enjoy Fetch will probably be thrilled if you offer to combine the two. Play at the beach, or choose a quiet lake or pond, and throw carefully: don't disturb wildlife or swimmers. This is a great game for older dogs who may be stiffening up a little: swimming doesn't strain their joints.

SAFETY

Make sure that what you throw is safe for your dog to fetch. If you live with a Fetch enthusiast, invest in a ball of just the right size for her to pick up and a "thrower" that will project it much further than would mere arm power. Small balls and toys, or sticks are all classic examples, but they're not ideal for throwing; if a dog gets overexcited she can choke on too small a toy, and sticks can splinter in a dog's mouth if they are grabbed too energetically.

▲ TWO As soon as your dog picks up the ball, say to her "Come." As she turns to move towards you, encourage her enthusiastically. If your dog then wanders off at this point, start again from the initial throw so that she begins to get the idea of a sequence.

▶ THREE When your dog returns to you, give the "Sit" instruction. As your dog sits she may naturally drop the ball, but if not, crouch down and offer her a treat in exchange. As soon as she drops the ball, praise her lavishly.

> ONE If you find that your dog is too excited to return the ball or toy you use for Fetch games, collect two toys she is equally fond of before you start. Throw the first and let her rush off to collect it.

Play it Again

Some dogs love playing Fetch so much that they become overexcited and refuse to give up the ball or toy that they've just retrieved. The easiest way to cure a dog of this habit while keeping the game fun is to exchange objects with her. This also helps to stop her from becoming over-obsessed with a single toy, and to understand the principle of exchange; if she knows that giving something up to you makes even better things happen, she's unlikely to get too possessive of objects that she sees as "hers." It will also help if she manages to get hold of something that she really shouldn't have, such as a shoe from your favorite pair. If she knows she's going to get something just as good in exchange, she'll be happy to give things up when asked.

USING "DROP"

If your dog is reluctant to give up her toys, teach her the "Drop" command. Place your hand gently under her jaw as she holds a ball in her mouth, then say "Drop" and carefully take the ball from her. Then give the ball back, so your dog knows that she won't be deprived of her toy just because she obeyed you.

▲ TWO As your dog picks up the first toy, call to her to catch her attention and wave the second in the air. Most dogs will run towards you; some will instantly drop the toy they're holding in order to grab the new one. If your dog isn't one of them, see the box on the left.

▶ THREE As soon as your dog gives up the first toy, throw the second one for her. While she's collecting it, retrieve the original toy, and, as she returns to you, repeat the sequence.

Go Get

Dogs can learn a surprising number of objects by name. Once you've taught your dog to recognize names, you can combine this with Fetch so that he can fetch different items from a selection. Don't try to teach him to distinguish between objects until he thoroughly understands Fetch. Then use a clicker to help him recognize specifics. Start with a particular toy nearby, encourage your dog's nose to it, while saying its name enthusiastically, then, as he turns to it, click and reward him. Repeat the name you've given the toy every time your dog noses it. When you're sure he understands, you can introduce more toys in the same way.

◀ ONE When your dog has learned the names of two or three toys by the means above, line up his favorites and name one: "Go get your ball!" He may pick up the wrong one a few times before getting it right. Repeat the name of the toy.

▶ TWO When he eventually picks up the right toy, click and reward him, giving him plenty of praise. Take a step back and ask him to bring the toy to you: "Come!"

▲ THREE As he turns towards you with the toy, make sure you praise him lavishly, and reward him when he brings it back to you. Let him play with his prize for a while, to show that getting the right answer makes good things happen.

KEEP IT SIMPLE

When first playing Go Get, make sure the toy you choose for your dog to identify is in plain view. If at any time he seems confused, go back to basics and start again: don't continue with ever-more complicated instructions.

▼ TWO It may take several attempts, but keep encouraging your dog and pointing to the newspaper. When he eventually picks it up, ask him to "Come."

▲ ONE Place the newspaper nearby, where your dog can clearly see it. You might want to try this one by the front door so that your dog can practice collecting the paper from the door mat. Give the command "Fetch Paper" and point to the newspaper.

Mail Carrier

Once your dog understands Fetch and Go Get, and can be relied on to bring objects back to you, you can introduce a bit more variety. Teaching him to fetch the morning newspaper or the mail is a trick that's useful for you as well as enjoyable for him. And if his interest in the mail carrier or other delivery people isn't as benign as you'd like it to be, giving him a job he enjoys to perform on their arrival may well discourage him from barking or other unwelcome behavior.

ON-TASK LEARNING

Don't start teaching your dog Mail Carrier until he fully understands Fetch, Come, and Drop on command. And don't be afraid to take any game right back to the beginning if your dog gets confused. Even telling him to "Sit" will come as a relief if he's muddled: following instructions that he's absolutely sure of will build his confidence, both in you and in his own abilities.

▼ THREE When your dog brings you the newspaper, say "Drop" and gently put your hand under his mouth to take the paper from him. Crouch down to his level and give him plenty of praise. Reward him with a treat or a favorite toy to play with.

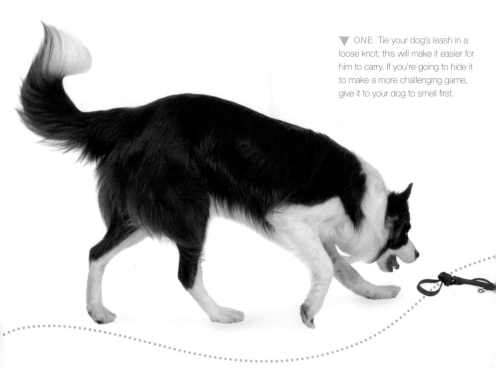

▼ ONE Tie your dog's leash in a loose knot; this will make it easier for him to carry. If you're going to hide it to make a more challenging game, give it to your dog to smell first.

Walkies!

Most dogs get excited in anticipation of their walk anyway, but you can build that excitement by giving them a job to do while you're getting ready. For your part, you may be putting on a coat, fetching a scarf, and donning your outdoor shoes. On his side your dog may only need his leash, but you can train him to collect it and bring it to you ready to put on. Getting his attention should be easy, as he's focusing on his walk, and you can use either "Walkies!" or "Fetch your leash!" as the key command. If your dog is already confident at Fetch games, you could vary things a little by hiding his leash as an additional step.

FIND THE ....?
|||||||||||||||||||||||||||||||||||||||||||||||||||

You can teach your dog a sequence of other things to fetch before a walk. Once he can bring his leash, practice "Where's my scarf?" or "Where's my hat?" and watch his excitement rise as he finds the extra item.

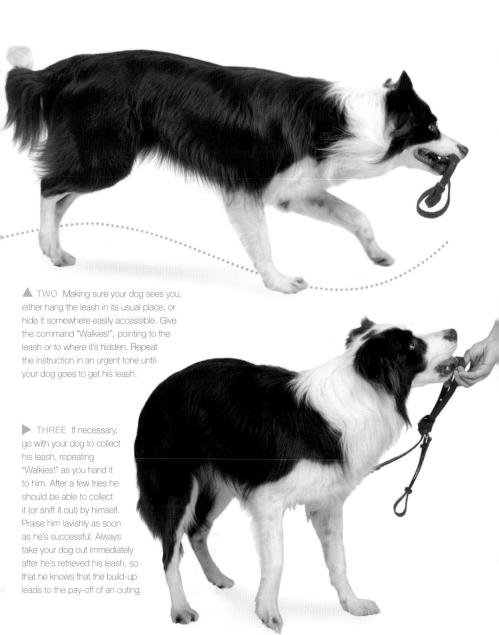

▲ TWO Making sure your dog sees you, either hang the leash in its usual place, or hide it somewhere easily accessible. Give the command "Walkies!", pointing to the leash or to where it's hidden. Repeat the instruction in an urgent tone until your dog goes to get his leash.

▶ THREE If necessary, go with your dog to collect his leash, repeating "Walkies!" as you hand it to him. After a few tries he should be able to collect it (or sniff it out) by himself. Praise him lavishly as soon as he's successful. Always take your dog out immediately after he's retrieved his leash, so that he knows that the build-up leads to the pay-off of an outing.

Give

To play this game you'll need to have mastered the "Drop" instruction; if you haven't, take a quick look at the box on page 24 before reading on. "Give" takes this one step further: it encourages your dog to give something up to you when you hold your hand out for it. It can't be overstressed that your dog must never feel she's losing out by obeying one of your instructions: her obedience must always seem worth it to her because of your praise, a treat, or a simple exchange of one thing for another (a treat for a toy, for example). When asking dogs to give something up, be careful of your manner, too; it should be bright, upbeat, and expectant, and never aggressive nor confrontational.

GENTLY DOES IT

If your dog really resists giving up the toy and starts to growl, don't raise your voice to her. Instead, give an audible gasp of "shock." This will have the element of surprise without alarming her, and you will probably find that she'll give up her toy.

◀ ONE When your dog has taken possession of a toy and is carrying it delightedly around, ask her to "Come." As she brings it to you, calm her a little—either by asking her to sit or saying "Good dog!" What you want next is for her to give up her toy without coercion, simply as you put your hand out.

▼ TWO Put out your hand, as you would for "Drop," but simply hold it next to the toy, rather than under your pet's chin. Say "Give" quietly, then, very gently, tug the toy to ask her to release it. If she pulls back, let the toy go, put your hand back next to the toy, and repeat the command. It may take a few attempts, but as soon as she releases the toy, praise her lavishly and treat her. Then give her back her toy.

Working
it Out

Hide and seek has always been a favorite game and here's how to teach the doggy version—your pet will enjoy it just as much as you do. Whether he's digging for hidden treasure (in his very own sandbox), coming eagerly to find you where you've hidden yourself, hunting out a squeaky toy, or following a scent trail, all these games require a little thought and a lot of enthusiasm. And while he may learn these games with the lure of a treat, soon enough whatever it is that he found through his own deductions will prove a sufficient reward for him to ask for a repeat run.

▶ ONE Start the game by familiarizing your dog with what's expected of him. Send a family member into another room and then say, "Where's John?" As you do so, have John call him from another room, and treat him when he runs next door to greet John. When he's confidently finding John whether he's called or not, it's time to give him a letter to deliver. Hand him the letter saying "Where's John?" again.

Direct Delivery

This game will teach your dog to deliver notes, letters, or small objects to anyone in the house. Keep the things he has to deliver easy for him to carry, and start with just one person's name. When, and only when, your dog has gone through the sequence above, you can start introducing other family members into the mix. Eventually—and with a good deal of practice—you'll have converted your pet into an in-house mail carrier, who can deliver the mail to each family member, wherever he or she is in the house.

NO CHEWING

Retrieving breeds tend to carry things gently: it's bred into them. Other groups, though, such as terriers or toy breeds, may find it hard not to chew and mouth whatever they're given to carry. You may find it necessary, therefore, to add a "no chewing" command to these dogs' repertoires.

▲ TWO As soon as the letter is safely held in your dog's mouth, have John call again from another room. At first your dog may drop the letter and rush to answer the call. If he does, pick it up and remind him to take it with him. Hand it to him again, saying "Wait ...," then "Where's John?"

◀ THREE As your dog arrives, get John to kneel down, hold out his hand, and say "Give." As soon as the dog hands over the letter, John should treat him and give him lots of praise. This is a relatively complex sequence to teach, so you may have a few false starts before your pet is successful. Be patient and keep the training session short.

Buried Treasure

A sandbox is enthusiastically welcomed into the play repertoire of many dogs. It's especially appealing to dogs that love to dig, such as most terrier breeds, and dogs that like to track scent will enjoy it too. The sandbox can also solve the problem of a dog that keeps digging up your flowerbeds: by giving her somewhere she can dig legitimately, you're allowing her to indulge her natural instincts in a suitable way. If your dog has ever been trained to use a litter box, she may not be able to distinguish between it and a sandbox—so pick another game! Cover the sandbox when you're not out in the backyard with your dog so that it doesn't become a magnet for the local cats, and the sand stays dry if there's a shower of rain.

▲ ONE In the previous game your dog watched while you hid the toy. Move things on a little in this one by showing your dog the toy, and then turning away (or running outside) to hide it in the sandbox.

▼ TWO The first time you bury a toy, leave a corner sticking out. Run with your dog to the sandbox, telling her to "Find the toy!" If she doesn't jump in and dig it up right away, indicate where it is with your hand.

THE RIGHT SAND

Make sure you buy the fine sand that is used specifically for sandboxes, not the coarser builder's sand. The latter can be very harsh and abrasive, and may scratch the skin of an over-enthusiastic digger.

THREE Found it! Now that your dog understands this game, you can introduce extra objects and bury them deeper in the sand. If she knows the names of several different objects, bury a few and ask her to bring you a particular one.

SAFETY Your sandbox should be a dedicated doggy sandpit, not one that children use too. Just as you would for a child's sandbox, check it for splinters or protruding nails before your dog first uses it.

FOUR When your dog brings you the object, ask her to "Give" as usual, then return the object to her—although you may find that she wants you to bury it again right away!

Squeak, Piggy, Squeak

Dogs are usually really enthusiastic about squeaky toys. "Squeak, Piggy, Squeak" is the perfect game when it's raining hard outside, and you have a houseful of people and a bored, underexercised dog on your hands. Several people together may enjoy this one, too, as your pet rushes from room to room eagerly seeking out the source of the noise. Try it with a variety of toys that make different noises—pet stores offer toys with a range of sounds, from a honking "duck" call to a high-pitched squeak like a mouse.

◀ ONE One "player" attracts your dog's attention with a squeaky toy. Everyone else who's playing takes a toy and hides in a different room around the house. You can conceal yourself behind the furniture or even in a closet if you want to increase the challenge for your dog. Then "squeak" your toys in unison, while the person with the dog tells him to "Go find!"

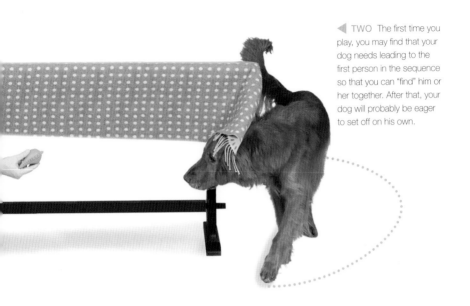

TWO The first time you play, you may find that your dog needs leading to the first person in the sequence so that you can "find" him or her together. After that, your dog will probably be eager to set off on his own.

THREE As he finds each new player, that person should congratulate and pet him, and hand over the toy, if he wants it—though he may be too eager to get to the next person to want it just then. Encourage him to keep going until all the toys and people have been "found."

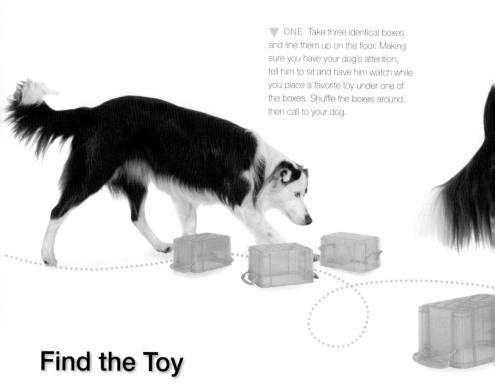

▼ ONE Take three identical boxes and line them up on the floor. Making sure you have your dog's attention, tell him to sit and have him watch while you place a favorite toy under one of the boxes. Shuffle the boxes around, then call to your dog.

Find the Toy

Once your dog has learned the names of different objects and can identify several of his toys individually, he may enjoy "Find the Toy." You can start with just two boxes, although we've shown three here. Not all dogs will be quick to turn the box over, so you may have to help a little when your pet has identified the right box; give him a chance to finish the game, but if he's not getting the idea, be prepared to keep showing him. As your dog masters this game, make it more difficult by using boxes that need to be opened, rather than just turned over. But never let your dog become frustrated by a game, or he will stop trying and it will become difficult to get him excited about anything new.

KEEP IT SPECIAL

Make sure that your dog associates the ingredients of the game (like these boxes) with the game, and the game only. Put the boxes away when you're not playing and take them out with an air of excitement; it will make your dog even more eager to join in.

TWO Tell him to "Find the toy!" He may take a few tries to get it right. If necessary, you can repeat the command while tapping the correct box with your finger. When he reaches the box, encourage him to turn it over and find the toy himself.

THREE As soon as your dog has the toy, ask him to bring it, then invite him to give it to you. Always return the toy to him as a reward.

Treat Trail

Most dogs will happily—and quickly—find a food treat if you hide one and indicate in its general direction; their sense of smell is strong enough to take them there. Little pieces of cooked chicken, sausage, or cheese are all perfect for this game, which is simply a pre-organized, extended version of Find the Treat! As always, be consistent with what you expect of your dog; if she's not allowed on the furniture, don't hide treats on the couch. Pick a room in which you're happy to have her freely roaming and nosing around for her Treat Trail.

▲ ONE Get your dog used to the idea of finding the treat by letting her sniff it, then tossing it away, just a little distance. Keep her on a leash if necessary, then let her go, saying "Find it." Then let her watch you place a treat somewhere she needs to nose it out—behind a flowerpot, perhaps, or in a storage box. Repeat "Find it" as she sniffs it out.

◀▲ TWO In the course of a few play sessions, get your dog used to waiting while you hide two or three treats before asking her to find them. Now the fun really begins. While she sits and stays outside a room, hide half-a-dozen treats in various places. Then let your dog into the room and excitedly tell her to "Find it!"

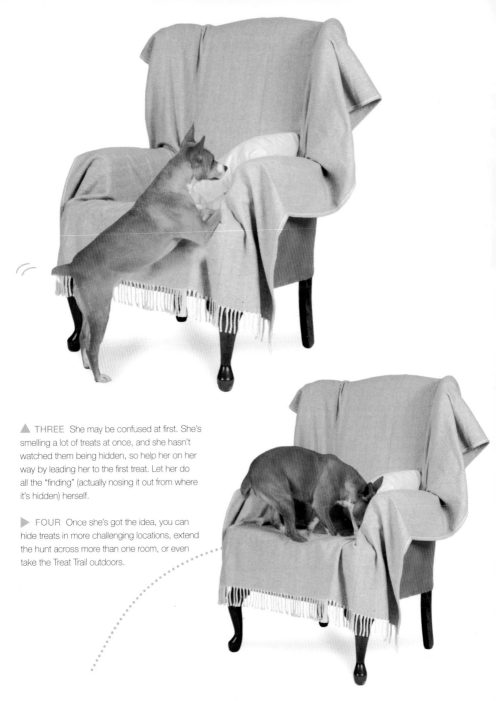

▲ THREE She may be confused at first. She's smelling a lot of treats at once, and she hasn't watched them being hidden, so help her on her way by leading her to the first treat. Let her do all the "finding" (actually nosing it out from where it's hidden) herself.

▶ FOUR Once she's got the idea, you can hide treats in more challenging locations, extend the hunt across more than one room, or even take the Treat Trail outdoors.

▲ ONE Sitting alongside your dog, gently roll a ball under a low table or chair. Join with her in looking under the table after it as it rolls.

Roll the Ball

Although it's obvious to you that you have to look at the whole picture before deciding which is the fastest route to get to something, it isn't obvious to a puppy. This young saluki-whippet cross needed two or three attempts before she figured out that the practical way to reach the ball wasn't necessarily the shortest. This is less of a game than an exercise; as usual, if you're challenging your dog, don't make the exercise too long or too frustrating at first; use a piece of furniture you can easily see around as well as under. You want your dog to figure it out, not to give up.

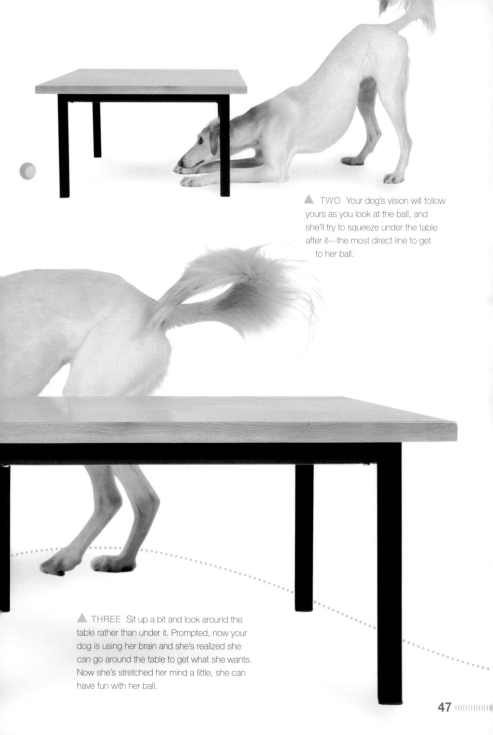

▲ TWO Your dog's vision will follow yours as you look at the ball, and she'll try to squeeze under the table after it—the most direct line to get to her ball.

▲ THREE Sit up a bit and look around the table rather than under it. Prompted, now your dog is using her brain and she's realized she can go around the table to get what she wants. Now she's stretched her mind a little, she can have fun with her ball.

▲ ONE Hide and Seek is the most fun when you're out walking with a friend. Have your friend sit by your dog and distract him, then walk away and hide behind a nearby tree or bush. Keep your hiding place quite obvious at first, and don't go too far.

Hide and Seek

Dogs enjoy "Hide and Seek" as much as people do, but a "find-me" exercise before playing the game for real outdoors will help your dog to get the point right away when you do go outside. To help him grasp the idea, put a treat into a small plastic cup or container, and call your dog from another room while rattling the treat. As soon as he arrives to claim it, praise him warmly. Try this exercise around the house, hiding further and further away, until he has to race through the whole house to find you. Then go through the steps above outdoors. And once your dog has grasped the principle, you can have two or more family members hide and your dog can "discover" you one by one!

▲ TWO As soon as you're hidden, call your dog, at the same time rattling his treat in a small plastic cup or container. Your dog will rush to find you, encouraged by your friend. As soon as he discovers you, give him his treat, then change places and have your friend hide. As you develop the game, you can make the hiding places more ambitious so as to offer your dog more of a challenge.

▼ THREE When your dog has learned the game, you can stop rattling the treat and simply call him. A big hug when your dog finds you will be enough of a reward for him.

Scent Trail

No dog is too old or too young to play this backyard game; even a very old and arthritic dog can enjoy following a scent trail at his own pace to reach a reward at the end. Unsurprisingly, scent hounds usually show the greatest aptitude for following a trail, but other breeds enjoy it too: practice with your dog and he'll soon get the hang of it. Make a "scent bag" to use by tying a few biscuits soaked in meat essence or gravy in a piece of cloth, and attach it to a piece of string so that it can be pulled along the ground.

STARTING YOUNG

Puppies are able to follow a scent trail from about three months of age. Try laying a trail for your pup, leading him to his dinner dish or a treat at its end.

▶ ONE While your dog is indoors, pull the scent bag along the ground in your backyard, laying a trail for your dog to follow. Don't pull it in a straight line; instead, make a winding trail going around trees and under foliage. Leave a surprise treat at the end of the trail for your dog to find.

TWO Bring your dog outdoors and hold out your fingers for him to sniff. Don't give him the bag itself; he'll simply try to eat the contents. Take him to the beginning of the trail and encourage him to start by bringing your hand down to the ground. As he lowers his head, he'll pick up the scent. If he seems confused, try leading him the first yard or two of the trail on his leash, pulling your fingers along the path of the scent.

THREE As your dog gets more confident about following a scent, make the trails more complicated, or lay a trail out in the woods so that you can play "tracker dog" together.

▲ ONE Stand still with your legs shoulder-width apart. Hold a treat ready in your left hand. Your dog needs to be on your left side. Lure him to the front of your left leg and encourage him through your legs by switching the treat to your right hand. Now lure him around your right leg.

Walk 'n' Weave

This game suits an active dog that loves a challenge. It's perhaps not surprising that many of the masters of "Walk 'n' Weave" and "Doggy Dancing" in the show ring are border collies, a breed that is famous for its smartness and agility. This game isn't for every dog, but most breeds can master it provided that you're consistent and patient while your pet is learning, and you don't persist in a session if your dog is getting bored. You should add it to your repertoire only when your dog has learned a number of other games and commands, and is used to working attentively with you.

▲ THREE Ready to walk 'n' weave? This one takes practice, so try it on your own first before trying to teach your dog. When he's on your left, lift your right leg. Don't forget your hand signals to lure him through! As your right foot hits the ground, lift your left leg and encourage him to weave around to your left side. Once you've both understood this move correctly try walking slowly forward.

▲ TWO At first, give the command "Weave," or use a clicker, but as your dog learns the game you can drop the command—and the treats—and use hand signals only. You'll need to lean down at first to reward him, but as you both progress you'll find you can stand up straighter and he'll still follow your movements easily.

TAKE YOUR TIME

|||||||||||||||||||||||||||||||||||||||||||||||||||||||||||||||||||||||||||||

This is a game for which you need a good existing rapport with your dog; it's not one for novices or puppies. Keep the sessions short, expect them to take a little time to learn, and don't let your dog get bored or confused. If you can both master this game, you've learned one of the basic moves for doggy dancing!

Trick and Treat

Your pet is a natural comedian—and you struggle to keep him busy. This section is for you. It offers a whole range of tricks that dogs that love playing to an audience will enjoy mastering. And, best of all, they're likely to summon an unsolicited round of applause. Some are harder than others, and a few are really difficult, but most dogs can learn to shake a paw, or give you a hug and a kiss, and those that are smart enough and persistent enough to learn Shy Dog or Night Night will have a party trick for life, with the likely added bonus of plenty of praise and treats.

▲ ONE Start by asking your dog to get into a "Down." Then kneel beside her and hold out your hand as you would to give her a belly rub. She will happily roll down on to one side.

Rollover

Most dogs find "Rollover" quite an easy command to obey, but before you start make sure that your dog is familiar with the Down command: don't try to make her roll over unless she is. If she's confused about what you want, she won't enjoy trying to understand you, and you may damage her confidence in the things she already knows how to do. If you're using the clicker method to help your dog learn, you should only click and reward when your dog is beyond the point of no return in her rollover!

SAFETY
Long-backed dogs, such as whippets and greyhounds, find rolling over more difficult than other more compact breeds. Don't persist if your dog looks uncomfortable.

◀ TWO Once your dog is lying on her side give her a brief belly rub, then produce a treat and, holding it over her ear, circle it slowly over her head. As you do so, say "Rollover." Some dogs find the movement very natural and will get the idea immediately, while with others it may take several tries. Reward your dog even if she hasn't managed a complete roll first time, then try again.

▼ THREE After a successful rollover, ask your dog to stand. When she's mastered a rollover confidently, try it without the treat, using just the circling hand signal, and treat her only on completion.

▼ ONE Your dog can begin from either a standing or a sitting position, whichever comes naturally. Start by crouching down next to him and asking him to go into a "Down."

▼ TWO As soon as he's down, give him the command to "Rollover." But—here's the clever part—just as he reaches the halfway stage, lying on his side, ask him to "Wait" and give him a treat. Once he's settled on his side, try the command "Play Dead."

Play Dead

This fits more into the category of trick than game, but no one who has seen a dog successfully performing it and subsequently receiving the praise that is his due could doubt that he enjoys it very much indeed. Although this trick is not especially hard to teach, it involves sequenced behavior, so you must ensure that your dog is familiar with both the "Down" and the "Rollover" commands before attempting it. And when he's playing dead successfully, don't expect your pet to stay in position for long when he hears the laughter and applause of an amused audience watching him perform!

▼ THREE Once he's got the idea—and it will certainly take a little practice—you'll eventually be able to drop the first two commands and he will simply flop to the ground when you say "Play Dead." If you want (and you're not troubled by accusations of tastelessness), you can introduce the hand signal of pointing your trigger finger.

▶ ONE The easiest way to teach this is to wait until your dog begins to stretch out his front legs naturally. As your dog extends his front paws, say "Bow," then praise and reward him. He'll be surprised at first, but when you've caught him mid-stretch and rewarded him several times, he'll start to get the idea.

Take a Bow

Watch your dog just going about his daily affairs and you'll notice that he stretches out his body and "bows" down over his front legs as part of his regular stretching routine, when waking from a nap or getting ready for some lively activity. If you're quick, you can catch your pet as he goes into a natural bow, give him the command, and treat him as he completes it. Many dogs like the position so much that they'll pick up the command very quickly. If this doesn't come naturally to your dog, take him through the steps above; he'll soon get the idea. Bow to him as you give the command, and watch him bow politely back.

SAFETY This isn't a game for an elderly, arthritic dog, or a dog with a bad back. If you haven't seen your senior dog adopting this position naturally for a while, don't encourage him to do it just for fun.

▶ TWO Next time he starts to stretch, place a treat just in front of his paws. At the same time, hold his tummy up with one hand and give the command "Bow." Dogs usually pick this one up quickly, and soon he won't need the support, and will be bowing when you ask him.

ONE Look closely and you'll notice your dog tends to use either her left or her right side more often. All dogs favor one side; it will be the side she takes off from when starting to move. Use this side to teach her. Begin by asking her to go into a "Sit."

Shake a Paw

This game comes naturally to most dogs. They use pawing a great deal in play and between themselves, and they often develop an annoying habit of pawing "their" humans when they want attention or a game. As well as being enjoyable for you to teach and your dog to learn, instructing your pet to shake a paw can help you to control pawing at other times when it's not welcome; by associating pawing with a specific command, your dog is less likely to do it unasked.

TWO Sit down in front of her and lightly touch the muscle of the shoulder of the paw you want her to lift. Her front leg will lift slightly, automatically. She won't need much prompting for this one; pawing is a natural behavior for dogs.

▼ THREE As her paw lifts, take it in your hand, shake it gently, and say "Shake a Paw." Use an underhand position; covering her paw with your hand can threaten a young or nervous dog. When she's confident shaking a paw, you can ask her to do it when you're standing in front of her.

WAVE HELLO

When your dog can shake hands on her own, you can extend the game by teaching her to wave. Stand back slightly as she holds out her paw. She will paw the air, and as she does so you can teach her the command "Wave Hello."

Clean Up

Tired of picking up after everyone in the household? Then "Clean Up" may be a useful trick to teach your dog. Just follow the steps and at least one member of the family will be clearing up after themselves. If your dog enjoys fast-paced games, then you can supplement Clean Up (when he's learned it thoroughly) with "Doggy Dunk." In this simple variation, you roll a ball towards your dog and ask him to "Clean Up." As soon as he pops the ball into the basket, you can roll another. Some dogs learn this one so enthusiastically that you'll have to work hard to keep up!

◀ ONE To help your dog learn this one easily, set the scene in advance by leaving his toy basket in a fixed place and scattering the toys that you want him to Clean Up nearby. Start the game by showing him one of his favorite toys and encouraging him to go with you to his toy basket.

▲ TWO Hand your dog the toy and encourage him to hold it in his mouth. Holding a treat in your hand, lure your dog over the basket, then offer the treat. He will drop his toy into the basket. As he does so, tell him to "Clean Up."

◀ THREE Practice using just one toy a couple of times a day until he's learned to Clean Up his favorite. When he's mastered this, you can increase the number of toys he picks up by giving him a treat only with every second toy put in the basket.

Catch the Treat

This is a hard trick for dogs to learn. Take it slowly, teach it in its component parts as shown, be patient, and praise any attempts that show that your dog is getting the idea, even if he isn't successful at first. Keep the sessions very short—no more than three or four attempts each time. Play an easy game with your dog in between learning sessions too, so that he doesn't become frustrated if he's finding "Catch the Treat" difficult. Make sure that you also stand back as you teach him to keep his nose still. Dogs find anyone, even a well-loved owner, threatening if they get too close while looming over them, and your pet needs to be concentrating on what it is that you want him to do.

▲ ONE Your dog needs to learn to keep his nose steady first. Hold his nose very gently, while offering a treat as a lure in your other hand, and ask him to "Stay." If he can't keep still, he won't be able to balance the treat. Once he's learnt this game you won't need to hold his nose, as your dog will understand that he needs to keep steady while you balance the treat.

▶ TWO When your dog is holding his nose steady, treat him, then, gently holding his muzzle, balance a small treat on top of his nose. (The dog in the pictures is a virtuoso and can toss quite large treats, but while your dog is learning, it's best to start with something small and light.) If he starts to move, tell him to "Stay." If he holds still for even a moment, praise him lavishly and reward him.

▼ THREE Now step back and make a sharp throwing gesture upwards with your hand. As your dog looks up at your hand—and dislodges the treat—give the command "Catch!" Eventually your throwing action will encourage him to flip the treat.

▼ FOUR The reward at last! You've probably had to persevere with a few attempts when your dog simply slipped the treat from his nose into his mouth, and with a few others when he looked up at you and dislodged the treat accidentally. Finally, though, he's got it—and this is a trick that will win him lots of laughter and applause when he performs it with a bigger audience.

▲ ONE Choose a suitable chair. If your dog is allowed on the furniture, don't use her favorite chair for this game: it should be your choice, not hers. Show her the chair, then ask her to "Come," and then "Up."

Jump Up

All fit and active dogs love to jump—and the real challenge with most dogs is to keep them *off* the furniture, rather than inviting them onto it. The game here is to teach your dog to jump up onto a chair of your choice, not hers, and at your request, rather than her whim! Choose a stable chair with which to practice on a non-slip surface, and don't play this game with an older or arthritic dog, or a very young one; puppies shouldn't be encouraged to jump too much while they're still growing, and their bones and muscles are still developing.

UP IN ARMS

You can also teach most dogs to jump up into your arms (although this may not be a trick you want to practice if you own a large breed). Ask her to "Stay," then walk across the room and give the commands "Come" and "Up," patting your knees as you do so. When your dog grasps the game, praise her warmly.

◀ TWO Praise and reward her when she jumps, then move away from the chair while asking her to "Stay." You're trying to teach her that she should only jump onto or off the chair when you say the word.

▼ THREE Wait a few seconds, then give the command "Down." Keep this game varied by changing which chair you choose. You can even make a game of deciding, "Hmm, let me see ...", looking back and forth, while your dog excitedly looks to you to see which chair you're going to pick.

Hugs 'n' Kisses

You probably already have a tactile relationship with your dog (most owners do), and you may find that she already hugs and kisses you of her own accord. Even if she does, it's nice to be able to ask for a kiss from someone who you're sure will be happy to oblige! This also has the charm of being an extremely simple game, because it's taught purely by reinforcing what a dog does anyway. It's easier to teach small dogs, because you can introduce your pet to the idea when she's already sitting in your lap. If you want to play the game with a much bigger dog, sit down alongside her before starting, so that your faces are on the same level.

▶ ONE Make sure your dog is sitting squarely on your lap so that she doesn't lose her balance.

SAFETY Don't play this game with a dog that has back problems or one with a long spine, such as a basset hound or a dachshund.

TWO Lift your dog's paws and gently place them on your shoulders while saying "Hug." You can also introduce a hand signal for Hug; simply cross your hands over your chest and tap your shoulders. Praise her as she moves in closer.

THREE When your dog moves to lick your face, say "Kisses" and praise her enthusiastically. When you've finished playing, always give the command "Down." If your dog is easily excited, end the game if she starts to get too boisterous, before the kisses become nips!

Talk to Me

Talk to Me is a worthwhile game for you to teach your dog, because it not only teaches him to bark when asked but also to stop barking. Quite a lot of behavior that can become a tiresome habit in an untrained dog can be reprogrammed in a trained one as a useful trick that is simply part of his extensive repertoire. Don't start to teach this trick when your dog is barking anyway: it will simply confuse him. Instead, pick a time when there are no other distractions and he can focus his attention exclusively on you.

◀ ONE Fetch your dog's favorite toy and hold it a little out of his reach. Call him until you're sure that his attention is focused on the toy or treat, and tell him to "Speak." He'll soon be frustrated enough by not getting access to his toy to bark. As soon as he does so, praise him enthusiastically. Tell him to "Speak" for other toys, or a treat. As soon as he barks, reward him.

SING ALONG

|||||||||||||||||||||||||||||||||||||||||||||||||||||||||||||||||||||||||||||||||||||||||||||

Many dogs like music; you will find that some will naturally burst into song when you play your favorite CD. If you have a singing dog, try performing a duet with him. It could be a good party piece for you both!

TWO As soon as your dog can bark on request, teach him to whisper. Hold a treat in your hand, say "Speak," and when he barks for it, say in a low tone "Shhh, whisper." You may have to do this a few times in a very quiet voice, and he'll probably try a range of barks, but when he eventually does a gentle, quiet bark, praise and treat him. He'll soon learn the difference between "Speak" and "Whisper."

THREE You can also teach your dog to keep quiet. Hold a treat in front of him, let him see it, and when he barks say "Quiet." Don't look at him. When he stops barking, give him lots of praise and the treat. "Speak," "Whisper," and "Quiet" are usually surprisingly easy to add to a dog's repertoire.

▲ ONE Crouch down in front of your dog and encourage her to stand on her hind legs by offering her a treat held slightly above her head. Use your left hand; this will make it easier for her to move clockwise. Your hand should be held palm-down.

▲ TWO Move the treat in a circle directly above her head. Be careful not to position your hand behind her head. She'll start moving on her hind legs to keep her treat in view. As she starts to move, tell her to "Jive" and reward and praise her.

▲ THREE Keep playing in short sessions and encourage her to move around in a circle by hanging on to the treat until she's taken a few more steps on her hind legs. Give the command "Jive" as she does so. Encourage her to dance a full circle, then reward and praise her again.

Doggy Dancing

Have you ever seen dogs dancing with their owners in show competitions or at agility contests on television? If so you will probably have marveled at the extraordinary coordination displayed. You and your pet may never get yourselves up to competition standard, but smaller dogs—especially toy breeds and terriers—often show a surprisingly natural aptitude for walking on their hind legs, and sometimes appear to enjoy adding quite elaborate turns. Make sure the floor you're working on isn't shiny or slippery, and that your dog has plenty of room to maneuver while you're practicing, then get the treats out, put the music on, and strut your stuff.

◀ FOUR Now you can teach her doggy pirouettes! After she's done one full turn, encourage her to continue by not handing over the treat until she takes a few more steps. Always stop the game before she tires of it, or gets frustrated.

SAFETY As you'd expect, dancing isn't really suitable for long-backed dogs. Small breeds usually learn it easily; if you want to teach a much larger dog to dance, you might want to attend a professional doggy-dancing class.

High Fives

Most dogs love this game, but keep in mind some dogs just cannot sit up on their hind legs, so if your pet seems at all unwilling, don't persist. If you've taught your dog to shake a paw (*see pages 62–63*), you used one hand and one paw. This game uses both hands and both front paws, but it's not really very different to teach. If you find that your dog quickly gets the idea but tends to paddle the air frantically, try to slow her down a little by stilling your hand movements and lowering your voice. Wait until your dog has happily mastered the moves before you try "High Fives" from a standing position, as you don't want her to feel overwhelmed by you looming over her.

SAFETY Don't play this game with very young, or older and arthritic dogs; it can strain their backs. Also remember that some dogs cannot sit up on their hind legs or simply find it uncomfortable, so don't persist with this game if your dog appears reluctant to learn it.

▶ ONE Crouch down in front of your dog and hold out your hands, palms down. Say "Paws"; keep your hands on a level with your dog's head, otherwise she'll jump up.

TWO Repeat the sequence, raising your hands a little higher each time and encouraging your dog to lift both paws to meet your palms. Add the command "High Fives." Don't persist if your dog can't balance, though. Big dogs can find balancing hard work.

THREE As soon as at least one of her paws makes contact with the palm of your hand, reward and praise her. Soon you'll be able to drop the command "Paws" and just use "High Fives." This game is quite tiring for your dog, so keep the sessions short and fun.

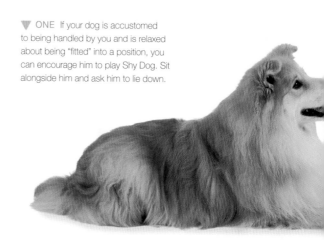

▼ ONE If your dog is accustomed
to being handled by you and is relaxed
about being "fitted" into a position, you
can encourage him to play Shy Dog. Sit
alongside him and ask him to lie down.

Shy Dog

This is a guaranteed crowd pleaser; no dog who has
learned it successfully will ever be short of a treat.
The easiest way to begin is to wait until your dog naturally
assumes a lying position with his nose tucked down
between his paws. You may have to help him along a little
if he doesn't often take up this pose. Whichever technique
you choose, never, ever force your dog into this or any
other pose. The way to develop your relationship with
your pet is to use the natural trust between you to coax
or treat him to do what you want. Coercion will always
be counter-productive: not only will your dog enjoy
playing and learning with you less, but you also risk
damaging his trust in you.

▶ TWO Take one of his front paws (you can ask him to "Shake a Paw," *see pages 62–63*), shake it, then place it gently across his other one.

▶ THREE Place your hands lightly behind his ears and position his head between his paws. Don't force him: if he's not relaxed about being handled like this, you'll have to wait for the Shy Dog position to happen naturally.

◀ FOUR Kneel down beside him, saying "Shy Dog," as you praise and reward his position. Some dogs are natural actors and will look coyly up at you from between their paws. Make sure he gets plenty of praise for his acting ability.

Night Night

This is another quite demanding trick. If your dog masters it he'll have every right to feel very pleased with himself, because it has several different steps. He'll need to be familiar and comfortable with the Play Dead game (*see pages 58–59*) before you start. As always with the harder tricks and games you're learning with your dog, keep your teaching sessions short, fun, and positive, and play some of the easier games in between. If your dog has a favorite cloth or blanket that he enjoys mouthing, incorporate it into the game, as he'll be used to moving it with his teeth.

▲ ONE Get your dog used to being covered with a blanket before you start teaching in earnest. Some dogs don't like being covered up, so it may take some time and patience before he feels comfortable. Then tell your dog to "Play Dead," and, when he's lying down on his side, cover him with his blanket.

▲ **TWO** Saying "Night Night," offer him a corner of his blanket, or place it gently in his mouth. Don't be discouraged if he jumps up. Just go back to the beginning. Only try this a few times, though, before moving on to something else. When he eventually takes his blanket in his mouth, praise and treat him.

▼ **THREE** When he's learned to grab his blanket, you'll eventually be able to bypass the Play Dead command and just say "Night Night."

Agility
Challenge

A dog that just seems to fly through the air when she's playing ball with you, and is always looking eagerly to you for guidance and instruction, is likely to be a natural agility athlete. This section guides you through all the different activities in a professional agility circuit and looks at how you can set up your own backyard version at home. If your pet is especially eager you may even find that you're doing timed rounds and joining a local agility class. Even dogs that aren't wild about the whole circuit usually enjoy one or two of the activities—if necessary, you can customize the course especially for your own pet.

Making a Backyard Agility Course

Many dogs love energetic play with lots of jumping. If your dog is like this, and has also demonstrated that he can figure things out for himself, you might want to consider building him his own agility course on which to practice. Take him to a local agility class for a few sessions, even if you're not interested in competing professionally; it will ensure you understand the proper use of the equipment and understand any safety issues. New equipment can be expensive, so look around for good second-hand items. If you decide to improvise, it's worth asking the advice of your agility class instructor, to make sure that the at-home entertainment center you're giving your dog is safe, as well as fun.

▲ ABOVE Jumping is a mainstay of agility trials. You can purchase professional jumps or improvise and build your own, just make sure they're not too high for your dog—he should be jumping no higher than his shoulder height.

SAFETY **If you're setting up a backyard agility course, make sure you've got enough space between obstacles. Jumps in particular need room for take off and landing—at least five strides for take off and four to recover.**

◀ LEFT Line up cones or other obstacles for your dog to weave in and out of. You can make this even more challenging for your dog by teaching him to dribble a ball between the obstacles.

▶ RIGHT A professional pause table is 36 inches square. It sits on a stand, which is adjusted to the height of the dog. In competitions, dogs have to pause on this table for five seconds before proceeding to the next obstacle. The table must be sturdy, with a non-slip surface.

▼ BELOW The overall length of a professional chute tunnel is between 12 and 15 feet. The entry and exit sections are made of rigid material so they don't collapse while the dog is barreling through. A children's play tunnel is adequate for novices.

▶ ONE Your dog will be jumping on her own in no time, but first you have to show her what to do. Put her leash on, and jog up to and over the jump. At the same time, say "Over." Give her lots of praise and encouragement. You may find that you have to jump on your own the first few times, while she holds back.

Starter Jumping

These pictures will make you reconsider any preconceptions you may have had about which breeds enjoy agility. The little papillon shown here weighs just four pounds, but she can do a complete agility course with equipment appropriately scaled down for her size. Not all dogs are natural jumpers, though, so take it slowly and always start with a very low jump; if your dog looks daunted by the recommended half-shoulder height, take it even lower, to just a few inches. You want your dog to be confident about jumping first, however low the jump is; when she's jumping happily, you can consider raising the height gradually.

FIRST OF ALL

Measure the height of your dog's shoulder and divide this by half. This is how high you should build the jump when first teaching your dog. A broom handle balanced between two boxes, buckets, or cones works well.

◀ **TWO** Keep on jumping until she understands the game, then jump alongside her until she's obviously happy about it. Now, stop just before the jump and she'll jump it by herself. Gradually stop further away from the jump, while still giving the command "Over." Eventually, you'll be able to just point and give the command.

SAFETY Make sure the jump you build is easily knocked over and is the correct height for your dog. This game is best played outdoors, but if you have plenty of space indoors then it can be a good game for rainy days: just make sure your dog is playing on a non-slip surface.

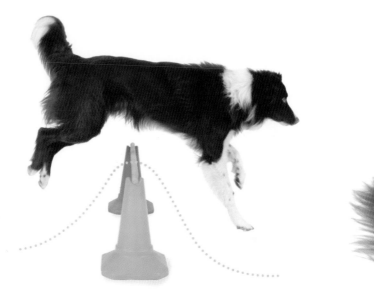

▲ ONE Just as when you were teaching your dog his first jump, help him when you start to add extra steps by taking the first jump with him. Then jog with him to the second.

Hurdles

When your dog has enjoyed mastering one lowish jump, you may want to introduce him to the joys of hurdling. Hurdles should be added one at a time: go from one jump to two, to three, and so on. Unless you have a really enormous indoor space (your own gym?) you'll need to set them up outside to ensure that your dog has plenty of space to clear each jump. Remember the golden numbers: five dog strides to approach each jump and four more to "recover" from landing. Always set hurdles up in a straight line too; you don't want your dog to strain himself by angling his position between one jump and the next.

▼ TWO Jump over the second hurdle together, then try the two hurdles again. As your dog's confidence grows, encourage him to jump alone, move further away, and use a hand signal to go with the "Over" command. Formal agility trainers use just the gesture, and, whether or not you want to develop your skills in class, you might as well train like the professionals.

SAFETY Don't play this game with a dog aged less than a year: young dogs' joints are vulnerable to strain.

ONE Hold the hoop steady at floor level, or just an inch or so off the ground. With your other hand, offer your dog a treat and tell him to come "Through."

Hoopla

Jumping through a hoop is a natural progression from taking a hurdle. Your dog may hesitate a little more before jumping because he's not sure about the idea of jumping through an "enclosed" space—even one enclosed by a barrier as insubstantial as a hoop. The lower and steadier you hold the hoop, the quicker your dog's confidence will build, and the easier he'll find the jump. If he continues to look uncertain about the idea, hop back and forth through the hoop yourself to give him some encouragement.

SAFETY **Never ask your dog to jump higher than the level of his shoulder; you risk placing too much strain on his joints and muscles.**

TWO Repeat the step, moving the hoop upward, an inch at a time. Say "Through" each time and soon your dog will be happily hopping through the hoop to get his treat.

THREE When your dog is happy to hop through the hoop, raise it just—only just—to the level at which he'll have to jump. Then throw a treat to the other side and say "Through." He'll probably jump without thinking. If necessary, you can block off the sides of the hoop so that he can't walk around it!

FOUR Once your dog is really accomplished at jumping through hoops, you can advance him to professional agility equipment, such as a tire jump.

91

▲ ONE Stand in front of your dog with a treat held in your closed hand. Your dog will try to take the treat, but on discovering that he can't he will back away.

Back 'n' Around

This can be taught as two separate games— walking backwards and walking in circles—or combined so that your dog learns to walk in reverse circles. First, you need to follow the steps above to teach him to walk backwards, then follow the steps on the right to teach the circle part of the routine. The easiest way to combine the two games is to take your dog around the obstacles face first, then ask him to do them backwards, accompanying him yourself as he does so.

TWO As your dog steps back, click and use the command, "Back." Praise and reward him with the treat you had held in your hand.

THREE Soon your dog will know to walk backwards when given the command, and over time you can increase the distance between yourself and your dog.

ONE To get your dog to walk in a circle, place an obstacle alongside him and lure him around it with a treat held in your hand as you give the command "Around." Reward him with the treat when he has gone all the way around the obstacle.

TWO You'll probably need to practice this for some time before your dog will do it without the lure of a treat. But once he can do it easily, you can combine the two moves and walk through the obstacles first forwards, then backwards.

▶ ONE Start with a short tunnel at first and make sure your dog can see through it. Tell her to sit at one end of the tunnel, and kneel down at the other end so that she can see you. Encourage her through.

Tunneling Out

Start this game with a short tunnel at first. If you're improvising, it can be as simple as an open-ended box, but make sure it's stable and won't move or collapse as your dog goes through. If she proves adept at this game and enjoys it, do invest in a proper play tunnel; they're the most inexpensive part of an agility circuit. The most common difficulty when teaching a dog the tunnel game is having her double back to the start when she's halfway through. You can avoid this by always standing at the tunnel's exit and calling her so that she heads towards your voice if she becomes uncertain.

◀ TWO As she exits the tunnel, praise her and give her a treat. Don't place treats in the tunnel itself, even at the beginning; you'll only be encouraging her to stop halfway through for a snack.

THREE As soon as she's confident in the short tunnel, add a section (but just a short piece at a time). Run towards it with her, saying "Tunnel." When she's happily running through the tunnel at its full extent, add a curve in the middle to make the game a little more challenging.

▲ ONE Start by placing no more than four obstacles in a straight line. Leave a space very slightly shorter than your dog's body length between them.

Slalom

This exercise is the first step in lots of weaving games, so make sure your dog has learned the basics correctly. Although you start with only three or four obstacles, you can quickly build up the number, and return through them with your dog until you've built up to a full circuit. The obstacles don't have to be cones. You could use old grocery boxes, or upturned buckets, but they shouldn't be too large; your dog needs to get a sense of the whole row and his place in it. As you practice, gradually pick up the pace; the ultimate aim is for you and your dog to be able to Slalom at a fast trot, and, finally, for him to manage the Slalom on his own.

▲ TWO Walking with your dog by your right side, bend slightly to the left and lure him between the first two obstacles with a treat.

BE PATIENT

||||||||||||||||||||||||||||||||||||||||||||||||||||||||||||||||||||||||||||||||||||

This game is the mainstay of all agility circuits, so it's worth getting it right. Be patient and calm, and don't expect your dog to learn everything at once. If you persevere, most dogs suddenly reach a point at which they get it, and are running through the obstacles. But this occurs naturally; it can't be forced.

▼ THREE Direct him back towards the right so that you both pass between the second and third obstacle, then back to the left to pass between the third and the fourth. As you reach the end of the "course," praise him lavishly and give him a treat.

Perfect Dribbling

This game is a combination of ordinary slalom and doggy soccer. Make sure your dog understands the command "Weave" before attempting to teach him to push a ball along the ground; trying to teach slalom and soccer simultaneously will overload even the brightest dog. Because this is one of the more challenging games you can teach, take it slowly and keep the sessions short to begin with, so that he doesn't get bored or frustrated before he masters the key skills.

▲ ONE Place a treat under a ball. Your dog will push the ball forward to get the treat. At the same time, say "Push." Repeat it a couple of times, then start to reward your dog only every two pushes. Be patient if he doesn't push the ball immediately. Leave it for a minute and start again.

THE RIGHT BALL

Make sure the ball you choose is fully inflated so that your dog can't pick it up in his mouth. It also needs to be strong enough not to suffer tooth damage! A basketball or soccer ball is a good choice.

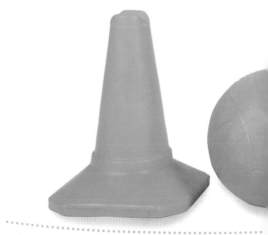

▼ TWO When your dog has got the hang of pushing the ball, set up a short course of cones. Start the game with his left shoulder nearest the first obstacle. Tell your dog to "Push" the ball and lead him around the obstacles, saying "Push, Weave."

▼ THREE You'll probably have to accompany your dog round the obstacles many times before he can do it on his own. Praise him and give him a treat every time he reaches the end of the course.

◀ ONE Make sure that the table is at a height she can easily manage and that the top is nonslipping. Place a treat in the center to lure her up, and give the command "Table."

"Paws" Table

Teaching your dog to stay put on a table until she's released by a gesture or a command is another mainstay of agility competitions. Even if you're not entering competitions, however, this is a good game to teach your dog, because it encourages obedience and concentration. She may find it difficult at first: most dogs are more used to being told to get down from instead of up onto furniture! But if you persist she'll learn the game in the end. This can also be a good calming exercise for particularly excitable dogs; the wait gives them a little "time out" to bring themselves under control.

TWO Your dog must remain on the table until you tell her to get down. Use the command "Stay." Don't expect her to manage a long wait the first time around; a couple of seconds is enough for her to get the point.

WARMING UP

If you have ambitions to enter agility trials, do a warm up with your dog, energetically chasing her around the garden before practicing the pause table. You will increase your dog's concentration and your chance of success.

THREE When you give the command "Down," she can jump off. Gradually build up the time your dog has to wait until she can manage a full ten seconds before you release her.

▶ ONE Start the game by saying "Ready, steady, GO!" in an excited voice, then start off around the course running alongside your dog as fast as you can. Although he already knows the course, you may find that he skips one or two stages in his excitement and eagerness to keep up with you.

Race Against the Clock

M ake sure that you and your dog are both in peak condition before you undertake to time yourselves around an agility circuit. Have a stopwatch and a friend ready, and warm up first with a brisk walk around the course. Then go around once, at a trot, checking to see that your dog can deal with all the obstacles. Finally, inspire him with an excited command and set off around the course together. Time yourselves first to get a best-out-of-three record, and then practice the aspects of the course that pose more difficulty to determine whether you can improve your time.

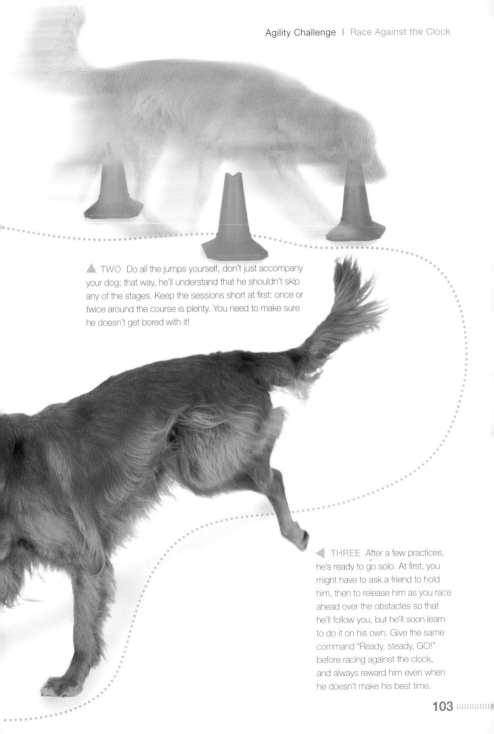

▲ TWO Do all the jumps yourself, don't just accompany your dog; that way, he'll understand that he shouldn't skip any of the stages. Keep the sessions short at first: once or twice around the course is plenty. You need to make sure he doesn't get bored with it!

◄ THREE After a few practices, he's ready to go solo. At first, you might have to ask a friend to hold him, then to release him as you race ahead over the obstacles so that he'll follow you, but he'll soon learn to do it on his own. Give the same command "Ready, steady, GO!" before racing against the clock, and always reward him even when he doesn't make his best time.

103

Group Agility

▲ ABOVE When it comes to agility, the breed or size of your dog doesn't matter, provided he or she is physically fit and able to undertake the course. A toy breed can have just as much fun as a border collie, for instance. And dogs learn from the example of other dogs—faster than you're able to teach them on your own.

From holding a play date with your dog and a couple of her "friends" to having them compete in your backyard agility circuit is just a small step. As long as they're all in good physical condition (and, ideally, not too different in size and shape, otherwise you'll have to modify the course between rounds), they will often enjoy the opportunity to be put through their paces with other dogs around. If you find the thought of several dogs all getting excited together in your backyard a bit too much to take, join a local agility class, where concerns of safety and organization can be resolved for you.

AGILITY CLASSES

||||||||||||||||||||||||||||||||||||||||||||||||||||||||||||||||||||||||||||||

If you're attending a group class, don't forget to take lots of treats and some favorite toys. If you're going to be away for some time, take some food and water. And don't forget to bring spare bags to clean up after your dog if necessary.

▼ BELOW Don't worry if your dog gets a bit excited. For her an agility course with other dogs is like a wonderful party with entertainment as a bonus. Having to process all the new experiences, she may forget some things. Be patient with her and start again if she gets confused.

Going Professional

Have you ever wondered whether you and your dog's teamwork would be good enough to demonstrate at a competitive level? Professional agility as a sport is growing at an annual rate of 10 percent a year—not bad when you consider the first agility trials were held in 1978 at Crufts in London. Dogs can start competing at about 18 months of age, and can keep going in special veteran classes until they're about 13 years old. If your agility training has been improving by leaps and bounds, begin by trying out your dog's and your own paces in a local agility contest, and find out how you do.

▲ ABOVE If you want to win, join your local agility club as soon as possible. This will accustom your dog to competitions and crowds, and you'll hear about all the trials in your local area.

TECHNIQUES & TRAINING

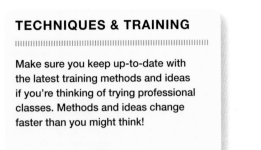

Make sure you keep up-to-date with the latest training methods and ideas if you're thinking of trying professional classes. Methods and ideas change faster than you might think!

▼ BELOW Border collies, Kelpies, and German shepherds tend to outperform most other breeds in the large dog trials. These breeds have the right body conformation and temperament. In the small dog classes, Shetland sheepdogs, poodles, and some breeds of terrier usually outperform the others.

Exercising
With Your Dog

I f you're enthusiastic about keeping fit, this section offers you plenty of ideas for exercising alongside your dog. Whether you love hiking, running, cycling, or team games the best, there's the possibility of bringing your canine companion along. With enough training time and encouragement, you can even teach your pet to play baseball or dog soccer. True, the games may not be quite as rigorous about the rules as the human versions, but you'll both still have plenty of fun.

Walking Together

The idea of leisurely country strolls with your pet may be one of the main reasons you got a dog in the first place. And no matter how many games you play with your dog, chances are that going walking will be the most time you spend together. Be aware of how fit your dog is: if he or she is elderly, injured, overweight, or has breathing problems, make the walk a slow, gentle one. Even leisurely walking helps with fitness—both yours and your dog's—and having a dog can motivate you to get out whatever the weather, and at busy times when you'd probably otherwise find an excuse not to go out.

▶ RIGHT Keep your dog on a leash if you're in a park or public space. Alternate walking and jogging is enjoyable exercise for both of you.

▶ RIGHT Go to different locations, walk a range of routes, and play a variety of games along the way. Walking is by far the best way to bond with your dog because it enables her to act in all the ways that come naturally.

SAFETY Have your dog wear a collar with an ID tag that gives your name and address on one side, and states that your dog is microchipped on the other (the latter fact may deter thieves). Get your dog microchipped: it's a minor procedure and an instant form of identification if she gets lost, and if somehow she also loses her collar and tag.

◀ LEFT For long walks, get yourself a pair of professionally fitted walking boots. Sneakers or galoshes won't do if you're scrambling up and down rough paths. Keep your dog leashed because you never know when you might have to pass through livestock or other dog hazards.

Running and Cycling

Running and cycling are both great ways to give a dog some challenging exercise beyond your usual gentle walk. A fit young dog will be able to keep up with you—and probably overtake you—on any running circuit, and many dogs enjoy running alongside cyclists as well. You'll need a few practice sessions to balance your pace with that of your dog's, particularly if she is running leashed and you're cycling; you don't want to race your dog at a pace she can't keep up, nor to be pulled along by your dog at a pace too fast for you. When you've got the balance right, either activity is good for the pair of you, and your dog will start to look on with excitement as you apply your fitness gear.

▼ BELOW Use your common sense. In any but the most remote situations keep your dog leashed, and start gradually with any running or cycling program.

SAFETY

Avoid the heat of the day; exercise early in the morning or during the evening. You may be able to "handle" hot weather, but even fit dogs may not; they can't sweat and compensate for high temperatures. Make sure fresh water is available for your dog along the way. Be extra aware of your dog during harsh weather, both in the heat and the cold—hot pavement can burn pads; ice and melting salt can also hurt or irritate pads. Pay extra attention to how much you feed your dog—don't let her do vigorous exercise after a large meal. Allow at least two hours between her meal and the exercise. Don't ask a young dog or puppy to run far; it can damage their joint development. If you're not certain that your dog is up to running with you, have her checked over by your vet.

◀ LEFT If you're cycling with your dog running alongside you on a leash, you might consider buying a springer. This is a special leash device that attaches to your bike and prevents you from being pulled over by your dog.

Hiking and Camping

Don't leave your pet at home if you're a keen hiker or camper. Some hiking trails and campsites allow dogs to come along, and your dog will love a break in routine with the chance of plenty of exercise as much as you do. Remember to bring along sufficient food for the trip; if you're somewhere remote, you won't be able to replenish dog food supplies. Think about where your pet is going to sleep, too. It will probably be best to set her up with a blanket or a travel crate in a corner of your tent at night; you don't want her pursuing the local wildlife across unfamiliar terrain in the pitch dark, so it's better for her to be safe inside.

▶ RIGHT You'll both enjoy your time away more if you've prepared yourselves with some training. A walk around the block is not the same as a steep mountain trail, so make sure both of you are fit enough before taking on long hikes.

▼ BELOW A trip away can be good for downtime as well as activity. Most dogs are thrilled just to spend time with their owners in the great outdoors, away from the duller aspects of their normal routine.

▲ ABOVE A fit dog with no back problems is able to carry up to 30 percent of his own body weight. A canine backpack is great for hiking. Get him used to the pack by loading it and putting it on at home, so he learns where his new shape will or will not fit.

LOCAL RULES

||||||||||||||||||||||||||||||||||||||||||||||||||||||||||||||||||||||||||||

Make sure you check with the local authorities what regulations apply in the area you've chosen. Your dog may be allowed only if he's leashed, and while that may be necessary for some dogs, it won't suit others.

SAFETY Make sure your dog is wearing suitable ID or is microchipped, in case you become separated from him. Always clean up after your dog. If you're staying in one of the camping sites that allow dogs, it's only considerate to your fellow campers. Don't forget to pack antibiotic cream and some bandages in case of an accident, plus parasite control, such as ticks, if applicable.

▼ ONE Let your dog see you play "human frisbee" first, then show him the frisbee and make some gentle throwing motions until he is excited enough to want to fetch it.

Frisbee Fun

Your pet may already love Fetch games, but Frisbee calls for a whole new catching skill. Before you start play in earnest, throw or roll the frisbee along the ground, giving the command "Get it" as you do so. Never throw it directly at your dog, always at an angle and parallel to the ground. Once your dog is catching a frisbee on the ground and returning it, try throwing it into the air. Kneel down and gently toss the frisbee to your dog. If he misses catching it, pick it up. Don't give the frisbee to your dog until he catches it, otherwise he'll consider it more as a passive toy than a form of exercise.

▼ TWO Start with at least two people as well as one dog! Gently throw the frisbee to the other human player. Your dog will quickly come between you and try to intercept the frisbee. Then you can do some throws specially for him.

THREE Once your dog has the frisbee, tell him to "Drop" it. As soon as he gets the idea that, just as with fetching a ball, every drop means another throw, he'll be keen to comply.

SAFETY Pick a fabric rather than a hard plastic frisbee; they're widely available and they won't hurt your dog's mouth. Don't play a frenetic, high-throwing game of Frisbee with an elderly or a very young dog; you may encourage him to overexert with a jump or twist too far. You can still play, but keep the game gentle.

▲ ABOVE Use a purpose-made Tug toy with knots on the ends. This is the simplest game of all: pick up the toy, let your dog make a grab for it, then simply tug on the other end. You'll almost certainly get tired of the game before your dog does!

▶ RIGHT Dogs will often naturally play Tug with one another. It's a game that provokes a lot of play growling and "yipping." Just keep an eye out to see that no one dog is becoming too possessive of that toy, and let the dogs enjoy themselves.

Tug of War

Dogs play "Tug" naturally: if you hang onto one end of something, such as a rope, even a very young puppy instinctively knows to grab the other end and start to pull it. Trainers used to recommend that owners didn't play Tug with dogs; they felt it reinforced the dog's natural possessive instinct and encouraged aggression. That's now held to be rather an old-fashioned view; provided that your dog will drop a toy when you request it, tug is an activity that is safe and enjoyable for your dog. However, make sure he doesn't become too intently focused. The signs of this are easily recognized. His body will stretch out and go lower, he will aim a fixed stare at his opponent, and he will look "frozen" in position; if this happens, break up the game.

SAFETY

If your dog becomes over-obsessed with getting the Tug toy, stop the game and take the rope away to give him a chance to calm down. This game is not suitable for young puppies if they're losing their baby teeth: it's best for them to fall out naturally.

Doggy Volleyball

A dog that has learned to push a ball for the slalom, may be able to master the skill of heading it back to you with his nose. This is quite a difficult game for any dog to learn, so be patient and, as always, keep your training sessions fun and short. You stand a better chance of success if you've noticed that your dog has often tried to join in human ball games: he's already looking at you and trying to figure out what to do. The hardest part for a dog is learning to "head" the ball with his nose, when his natural impulse is to catch it in his mouth. To teach your dog volleyball you'll need a net (a children's tennis or badminton net is suitable) and a soft ball. The ball should not be too large, but big enough for him to be able to follow easily; a size just a little larger than a tennis ball is ideal.

▲ ONE Your dog needs to be familiar with the Push command before you start (see pages 98–99). Get him to stand behind a low net; to begin with, this should be at a level no higher than his neck. Gently throw a small, soft ball just above his head and give the command "Push."

▶ TWO Your dog will need time to understand how to push the airborne ball with his nose, but he'll eventually make the connection. There are no short cuts in this game; your dog has to figure out for himself that he's supposed to bounce the ball on his nose, not take it in his mouth. Don't worry about whether he gets it back over the net or not. In the early stages of learning, it's quite enough that he learn to "head" the ball from his nose. Praise and treat him each time he manages it.

◀ THREE Patiently repeat the
command "Push" as you throw
the ball. Once he's learned to
bounce it on his nose, you can
encourage him to aim it at you,
back over the net.

▶ ONE Mark out your diamond in the park and divide into two teams. Your dog will always be on the fielding team. Give him a few human teammates (if possible) so he doesn't get too exhausted and they're there to help if he loses track of what he's supposed to do in the excitement of the game.

Doggy Baseball

What this game may lack in formal baseball skills and rules it will make up for in noise and fun. You may find it impossible to get your dog to follow the rules as the game hots up and he becomes more and more excited, but it's an invaluable opportunity for him to take part in a team game. You can play it with any number of people—you need at least two, one to pitch and one to bat—and any size or shape of enthusiastic dog. Your dog, naturally, is invariably with the fielding team. If he gets too overwrought to fetch the ball on his own, have a designated player run along with him.

IMPROVISE

Teams usually field at least four people for this game. If you don't have that many, you can try having just a batter, a pitcher, and your dog as chief fielder, and enjoy a game in the backyard rather than in the park.

SAFETY Use a light plastic bat and a soft ball for this game, never real baseball equipment: it's far too heavy and dangerous for a game in which your dog is involved.

◀ TWO As the batter hits the ball and runs to first base, the first-base fielder should ask your dog to fetch the ball. Quickly! If your dog is a good sprinter, you might get the other team "out" faster than you think. As more batters enter the game, the other base-fielders can call "Fetch."

▲ THREE Arm every fielder with a few treats so that they can reward your dog when he brings them the ball. As he gives up the ball ("Drop!") he should get a treat and plenty of praise.

▶ ONE Set up a "goal" with two cones, and stand between them with your legs apart. Call your dog, show him the ball, and encourage him to push it through your legs, giving the command "Push."

Soccer Games

Once your dog has learnt the Push command (*see pages 98–99*) and is pushing the ball confidently, it's time to add some variations to that newfound skill. When you play soccer with your dog, make it a game exclusively for him. If you involve him in human soccer, he's likely to try to join in with any soccer game he sees, and that will make him unpopular in the park. Instead, pick an appropriate ball (most real soccer balls are too heavy unless you have a very large, strong dog) and try a bit of goal scoring. If your dog gets very excited at the beginning, you may want to play a little Fetch and Catch with him first to take the edge off his excitement to the point at which he's able to concentrate.

THE BEST BALL

You'll need a ball that is too big for your dog to carry, and fully inflated, so that he can't bite it. It should also be light enough not to damage an enthusiastic canine player's nose!

▲ TWO Don't be tempted to place a treat behind your feet: your dog will simply go straight for the treat and forget the ball. Just persist, keeping the sessions short, and praise and treat your dog each time he aims that push accurately. As he begins to understand the game, you could teach "Shoot!" as an extra command.

◀ THREE When he's learned to get the ball past you, into the goal, reverse the roles to make the game more challenging. Encourage your dog to sit between the cones and push the ball back to you as you dribble it towards him. Finish the session with a game of "Chase the Ball" as a final bit of high-spirited fun for your dog.

Index

Acknowledgments

vy Press would like to say a big thank you to Nick Ridley for his excellent photography and all at Hearing Dogs for Deaf People (www.hearingdogs.org.uk) for being so helpful. Thank you especially to Jenny Moir and the dog handlers and owners that offered their time and assistance at the photo shoots, and of course to all the dogs, who couldn't have performed better or been more delightful to work with.

Tweed   Samba   Brock   Tia   Scooby   Tawny

Kai   Scout   Alice   Odele   Mole   Taggie

George   Mitch   Kia   Tabby   Mouse   Loki

Tyke   Fizz   Teal   Jake